Welcome the Baby Jesus

This edition published by
Concordia Publishing House
3558 S. Jefferson Avenue
St. Louis, MO 63118-3968

ISBN 0-7586-0249-9

© Copyright text: Margaret Barfield 2002
Copyright © illustrations: Joy Hutchinson
First published 2002 by
Scripture Union, 207–209 Queensway, Bletchley, Milton Keynes, MK2 2EB England
Web site: www.scriptureunion.org.uk

1 2 3 4 5 6 7 8 9 10   11 10 09 08 07 06 05 04 03 02

Printed and bound in Singapore

Welcome the Baby Jesus

Maggie Barfield

Illustrated by

Joy Hutchinson

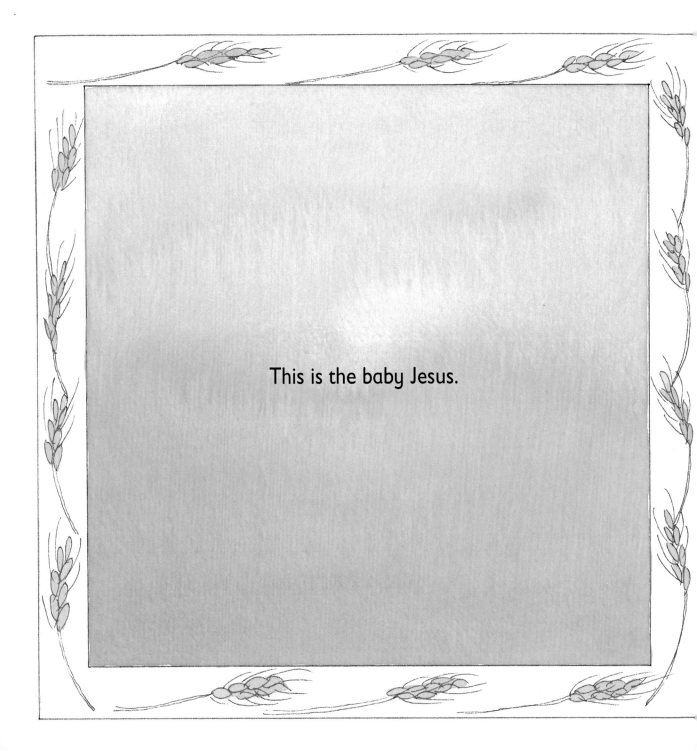

This is the baby Jesus.

This is the stable, a warm place to stay,
That was home for the baby Jesus.

This is Mary, loving and kind,

Who came to the stable, a warm place to stay,

That was home for the baby Jesus.

This is Joseph, patient and good,

Who took care of Mary, loving and kind,

Who came to the stable, a warm place to stay,

That was home for the baby Jesus.

This is the town called Bethlehem,
In the land of Joseph, patient and good,
Who took care of Mary, loving and kind,
Who came to the stable, a warm place to stay,
That was home for the baby Jesus.

These are the sheep that lived on the hill,

Above the town called Bethlehem,

In the land of Joseph, patient and good,

Who took care of Mary, loving and kind,

Who came to the stable, a warm place to stay,

That was home for the baby Jesus.

These are the shepherds on a cold, dark night,

Who guarded the sheep that lived on the hill,

Above the town called Bethlehem,

In the land of Joseph, patient and good,

Who took care of Mary, loving and kind,

Who came to the stable, a warm place to stay,

That was home for the baby Jesus.

These are the angels who sang with delight,
Who sang for the shepherds on a cold, dark night,
That guarded the sheep who lived on the hill,
Above the town called Bethlehem,
In the land of Joseph, patient and good,
Who took care of Mary, loving and kind,
Who came to the stable, a warm place to stay,
That was home for the baby Jesus.

These are the shepherds who ran down the hill,
When they heard the angels who sang with delight,
Leaving the sheep that lived on the hill,
Down to the town called Bethlehem,
To meet with Joseph, patient and good,
To see mother Mary, loving and kind,
Into the stable, a warm place to stay,
And worship the baby Jesus.

This is the star, which shone in the sky,
A star for the baby Jesus.

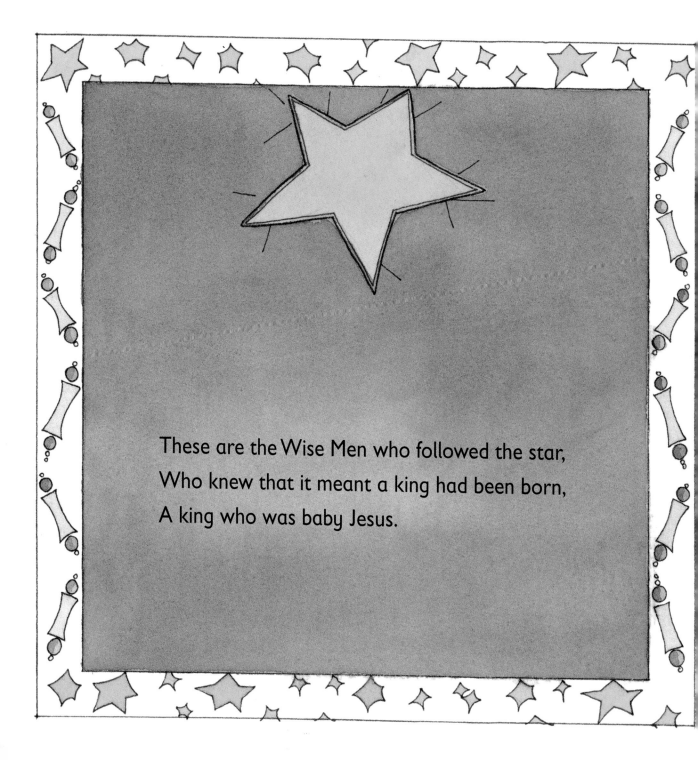

These are the Wise Men who followed the star,
Who knew that it meant a king had been born,
A king who was baby Jesus.

These are the camels that walked many miles,
Bringing the Wise Men who followed the star,
Who knew that it meant a king had been born,
A king who was baby Jesus.

This is the perfume, the gold, and the myrrh,
Carried by camels that walked many miles,
Given by Wise Men who followed the star,
Who knew that it meant a king had been born,
A king who was the baby Jesus.

These are the people all over the world,
For whom Jesus came as God's only Son,
Who sing and rejoice with hearts full of thanks,
To welcome the baby Jesus.

"For God so loved the world that He gave His one and only Son, that whoever believes in Him shall not perish but have eternal life." (John 3:16)